© Aladdin Books Ltd 2001

Designed and produced by
Aladdin Books Ltd
28 Percy Street
London W1P 0LD

*First published in
the United States in 2001 by*
Copper Beech Books,
an imprint of
The Millbrook Press
2 Old New Milford Road
Brookfield, Connecticut 06804

ISBN 0-7613-2463-1 (lib. bdg.)
ISBN 0-7613-2298-1 (paper ed.)

*Cataloging-in-Publication data is on
file at the Library of Congress*

Printed in Belgium

Coordinator
Jim Pipe

Design
Flick, Book Design and Graphics

Picture Research
Brian Hunter Smart

Illustration
Mary Lonsdale for SGA

Picture Credits
Abbreviations: t – top, m – middle,
b – bottom, r – right, l – left, c – center.
All photographs supplied by
Select Pictures except for:
Cover, 4tl, 6tl, 9, 10tl, 13, 14tl, 15, 20b,
21, 22b, 23ml, 24 all – Digital Stock. 2tl,
5b, 19, 23tr – Corbis/Royalty Free. 7, 10-
11, 16tl, 22mr – Corbis. 8tl – Roger
Vlitos. 20tl, 23br – John Foxx Images.

Hot and Cold

By Dr. Alvin Granowsky

Copper Beech Books
Brookfield, Connecticut

Hot and cold

Sonya and Greg are at the animal park. There are lots of animals.

Some animals like hot places, and some like cold places.

Greg and Sonya can't wait to see them all!

Hot

What is hot?

Today the sun is hot.

Sonya and Greg stand in the sun.

They feel very hot.

The sun is too hot for Sonya,
but not for the camels.

Camels live in a desert.
They stand in the sun all day.

Cold

What is cold?

That water is cold.

It makes Greg shiver.

But the seals love it!

If you jump in the sea on a hot day, it feels very cold!

Getting warm

What is warm?

Warm is a little hot.

Greg sits in the sun to get warm.

So does a crocodile!

In winter, this fox has fur to keep it warm. Greg and Sonya have winter coats to keep them warm.

Staying cool

What is cool?

Cool is a little cold.
When hippos get too warm,
they cool off in the water.

People can stay cool in a
swimming pool.

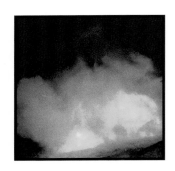

Fire

What is very hot?

Fire is very hot. Sonya and Greg eat hot dogs cooked on a fire.

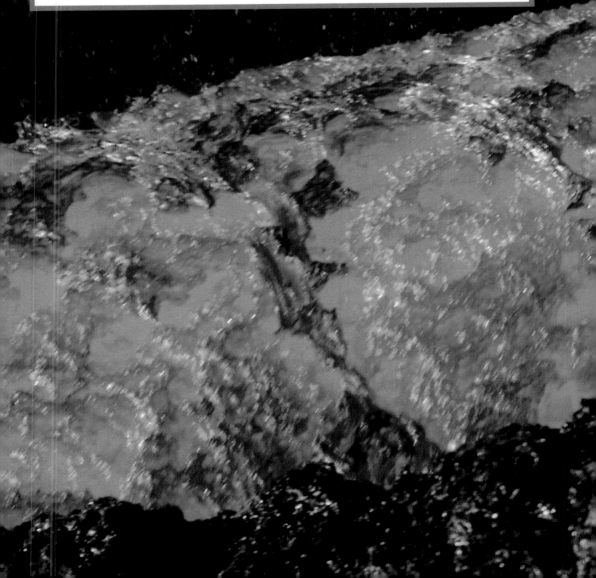

When rocks get very,
very hot, they melt.
They glow like fire!

Ice

What is very cold?

When water gets very cold, it turns into ice. When ice gets warm, it turns into water!

14

The penguin house is very cold. Penguins live on the ice. They swim in the icy water. Brrrr!

Warm and damp

At the animal park there is a rain forest hall.

Water drips from the trees and flowers. Bright birds call.

Sonya and Greg feel warm and damp.

Wind

What is cool and dry?

The wind blows and makes
Sonya and Greg feel cool.
Indoors, a fan makes a wind!

The wind makes things dry, too.

These towels are drying in
the wind.

Just right

Today the sun was hot.

The rain forest was hot and damp.

The pool water was cold.

The penguin house was very cold.

Sonya and Greg rest under a tree.
Here they are not too hot and
not too cold.

They are just right!

Here are some words about heat.

Hot

Cold

Warm

Cool

Icy

Here are some hot and cold things.

Desert

Popsicle

Fire

Sun

Pool

Can you write
a story with
these words?

Do you know?
When things get
hot or cold, they
change. Look what
happens to water!

When water
gets very cold,
it turns to ice
and snow.

When water gets
very hot, it boils.
It turns to steam.